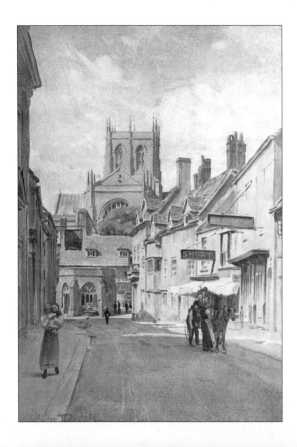

DORSET
RECIPES

compiled by
Amanda Persey

with paintings of
Thomas Hardy's Dorset
by Walter Tyndale

SALMON

Index

Cover pictures *front:* Puddletown *by E. W. Haslehurst*
back: Swanage Bay *by E. W. Haslehurst*
Title page: Sherborne *by Walter Tyndale*

Dorset Fair Gingerbreads

Crisp ginger biscuits such as these were usually on sale at Dorset Fairs.

3 oz butter, softened
3 oz soft brown sugar
4 tablespoons golden syrup, warmed

6 oz plain flour
1 level teaspoon baking powder
1 level teaspoon bicarbonate of soda

1 rounded teaspoon ground ginger

Set oven to 400°F or Mark 6. Cream together the butter and sugar in a bowl and add the golden syrup, flour and all other dry ingredients. Mix well to form a firm dough. Roll out on a lightly floured surface, cut out and form into about 30 small balls and place 4 inches apart on greased baking sheets. Cook for about 10 minutes until golden brown. Cool slightly before transferring to a wire rack.

West Street, Corfe Castle
"Corvesgate". A scene in the *Hand of Ethelberta*

Dorset Wiggs

These rich, spiced buns are traditionally served at breakfast time.

1 lb. strong white plain flour
Pinch each of ground cloves, mace and nutmeg
1 teaspoon caraway seeds (optional)
2 oz. butter, softened   2 oz. caster sugar
½ oz. fresh yeast   ½ pint milk, warmed
1 medium egg

Set oven to 400°F or Mark 6. Put the flour and spices, with the caraway seeds if desired, into a large bowl. Rub in the butter and stir in the sugar. Mix the yeast to a smooth cream with a little of the warm milk. Add the yeast mixture, the egg and enough of the remaining milk to mix to make a soft, elastic dough. Cover and leave to rise in a warm place for approximately 1½ hours until doubled in size. Shape into 6 large flat buns, put on to floured baking sheets and leave to rise again for 20 minutes. Cook for about 25 minutes until pale golden. Transfer to a wire rack and serve cold, sliced and buttered.

Cider Baked Pears

This simple recipe is a good way of serving the hard, cooking pears found in many Dorset country gardens.

1 oz soft brown sugar   ½ pint medium dry cider
6 pears, peeled, halved and cored
1 oz butter
Chopped walnuts for sprinkling

Set oven to 350°F or Mark 4. In a saucepan, dissolve the sugar in the cider over a low heat, bring to the boil and cook for 5 minutes to make a syrup. Arrange the pears in an ovenproof dish and pour the cider syrup over them. Dot with butter, cover and cook in the oven for 30 to 40 minutes until the pears are tender. Cool, sprinkle with walnuts and serve with clotted cream.

Shearer's Stew

A lamb stew finished with a topping of bread slices.

3 tablespoons cooking oil   1 oz butter
1½ lb leg of lamb, trimmed and cut into 1 inch cubes
2 onions, peeled and thinly sliced
1 oz plain flour   ½ pint brown ale   ½ pint lamb stock
2 carrots, peeled and sliced   Salt and pepper
4 thick slices of fresh white bread, cut into triangles

Set oven to 350°F or Mark 4. Heat the oil in a frying pan, add the butter and, when hot, brown the lamb in small batches and transfer to a casserole dish. Add the onions to the frying pan and cook gently until soft. Stir in the flour and cook for 2 to 3 minutes. Remove from the heat and stir in the brown ale and stock. Return to the heat and, stirring, bring to the boil. Add the carrots and seasoning to the meat in the casserole. Pour the liquid over all, cover and cook for 1 hour. Remove from the oven and stir well. Dip the bread slices into the liquid and arrange attractively on top. Return to the oven, uncovered, and cook for a further 30 minutes. Serves 4 to 6.

Steak and Oyster Pie

The flavour of this pie will be improved if the meat filling is cooked the day before.

1 tablespoon cooking oil   1 oz butter
1½ lb braising steak, cut into 1 inch cubes
1 medium onion, peeled and diced
2 tablespoons plain flour   ½ pint beef stock   ¼ pint red wine
1 tablespoon tomato purée   ½ teaspoon dried mixed herbs
1 small tin smoked oysters (drained)   8 oz puff pastry

Set oven to 325°F or Mark 3. Heat the oil in a large frying pan, add the butter and fry the beef in small batches until browned, and transfer to a casserole dish. Fry the onion gently until soft and lightly browned. Stir in the flour and cook for 2 to 3 minutes. Remove from the heat and add the stock, wine, tomato purée and herbs. Return to the heat and, stirring, bring to the boil. Pour over the meat, cover and cook in the oven for 1½ hours. Stir in the oysters and cook for a further 30 minutes. Next, transfer the meat to a 3 pint pie dish and insert a pie funnel in the centre. Roll out the pastry on a lightly floured surface and use to cover the pie dish. Trim and decorate. Increase oven to 425°F or Mark 7. When hot, cook the pie for 25 minutes then reduce oven to 350°F or Mark 4 and cook for a further 15 minutes. Serves 4 to 6.

Cottages at Sutton Poyntz
"Overcome" in *The Trumpet Major*

Sorrel Soup

A light, green-coloured soup; if sorrel leaves are not available spinach makes a good substitute.

1 oz butter	1 lb fresh sorrel (or spinach) leaves
1 onion, peeled and diced	1 tablespoon lemon juice
1 oz plain flour	Salt and pepper
1½ pints chicken stock	Single cream for swirling

Paprika for sprinkling

Melt the butter in a large saucepan, add the onion and cook gently until soft. Stir in the flour and cook for 2 to 3 minutes. Remove from the heat and add the chicken stock. Add the sorrel (or spinach) leaves, return to the heat and cook for 5 minutes. Purée in a food processor or liquidizer, return to the pan and flavour with lemon juice and season with salt and pepper. Re-heat and serve hot with a swirl of cream in each bowl and a sprinkling of paprika.

Charminster Curd Tart

Somewhat similar to a cheese-flavoured Bakewell tart.

8 oz shortcrust pastry	**3 eggs, separated**
8 oz curd cheese	**Grated rind and juice of one lemon**
2 oz ground almonds	**2 oz sultanas**
2 oz caster sugar	**1 oz chopped mixed peel (optional)**
¼ pint double cream	

Set oven to 400°F or Mark 6. Grease an 8 inch loose-bottomed flan tin. Roll out the pastry on a lightly floured surface and use to line the tin. Prick the pastry base with a fork, cover with foil pushed into the tin and bake for 15 minutes. Remove the foil. Soften the cheese with a wooden spoon in a large bowl and mix in the almonds, sugar and egg yolks. Stir in the lemon juice, rind, sultanas, peel (if desired) and cream. Whisk the egg whites until they form soft peaks and fold into the mixture with a metal spoon. Reduce oven to 350°F or Mark 4. Pour the mixture into the pastry case and bake for 45 to 55 minutes until golden in colour and firm to the touch. Serve warm or cold.

Affpuddle, near Dorchester
"East Egdon" in *The Return of the Native*

Potato Scones

A savoury scone which uses up left-over mashed potato.

9 oz self-raising flour   **3 oz butter, softened**
½ teaspoon salt   **6 oz mashed potato**
3 tablespoons milk

Set oven to 425°F or Mark 7. Put the flour and salt into a bowl. Rub in the butter and add the mashed potatoes. Add enough milk to mix to a soft dough. Turn on to a lightly floured surface and roll to ½ inch thickness. Cut into 12 to 15 even-sized triangles. Transfer to a floured baking sheet and cook for 10 minutes. Serve split and buttered, warm or cold.

If left-over mashed potato is not available, boil a sufficient quantity of peeled potatoes and mash.

Lemon Pork

Medallions of pork simmered in a sweet and sour sauce.

1 oz butter   1 medium onion, peeled and diced
1½ lb pork tenderloin, cut into ½ inch rounds
½ pint chicken stock   Rind and juice of one lemon
1 oz soft brown sugar
1 tablespoon Worcestershire sauce   1 oz sultanas
1 tablespoon cornflour (mixed with enough water to make a thin cream)
6 spring onions, trimmed and sliced

Melt the butter in a large frying pan and cook the onion gently for 5 minutes. Add the pork and brown the rounds on either side. Add the stock, lemon rind and juice, sugar, Worcestershire sauce and sultanas and simmer until the pork is tender; approximately 15 minutes. Stir in the cornflour liquid and lastly the spring onions. Bring to the boil and cook for a further 5 minutes. Serve hot with jacket potatoes and green vegetables. Serve 4 to 6.

Wessex Pasties

A conveniently portable meal which can be eaten hot or cold.

1½ lb. shortcrust pastry

FILLING
1 lb. braising steak, trimmed and coarsely minced or cut into small pieces
8 oz. potatoes, peeled and diced   4 oz. turnip, peeled and finely diced
1 medium onion, peeled and diced
Salt   Freshly ground black pepper

Set oven to 425°F or Mark 7. Mix together the filling ingredients in a bowl and season well. Divide the pastry into 8 pieces and roll out on a lightly floured surface into rounds about 8 inches in diameter (use a saucepan lid as a cutter). Divide the filling equally between the pastry rounds and damp the edges with water. Fold the pastry over and seal well, fluting the edges with the fingers. Place on a lightly floured baking sheet and cook for 20 minutes; reduce oven to 350°F or Mark 4 and cook for a further 45 minutes, covering the pasties with greaseproof paper if they begin to brown too much.

Moonshine

A rich version of a traditional bread and butter pudding.

2 oz butter, softened
6 thin slices white bread (crusts removed)
2 oz sultanas 2 oz caster sugar
3 eggs, beaten
¾ pint milk ¼ pint single cream
Grated rind of half a lemon
Freshly ground nutmeg

Set oven to 350°F or Mark 4. Use a little of the butter to grease a shallow ovenproof dish, and use the rest to butter the bread generously. Cut the bread into strips and arrange in the dish in layers, buttered side up, sprinkled with sultanas and sugar, finishing with a layer of buttered bread. Beat the eggs in a bowl. Heat the milk and cream in a pan to just below boiling point and stir into the eggs; add the lemon rind. Pour over the bread, sprinkle with nutmeg and leave to stand for 20 minutes for the bread to get well soaked. Bake for 30 to 40 minutes until the custard is set and the top is crisp and golden.

The Tithe Barn, Abbotsbury
Scene of the sheep shearing in *Far from the Madding Crowd*

Ham and Pea Soup

A sustaining soup with lots of flavour; ideal as a light luncheon dish.

1 oz butter   1 medium onion, peeled and diced
8 oz potatoes, peeled and diced
12 oz peas, podded (or use tinned garden peas)
1½ pints chicken stock
8 oz gammon, grilled and cut into small pieces
Pepper   Pinch each dried sage and thyme

Melt the butter in a large saucepan, add the onions and potatoes, cover and cook gently for 10 minutes, stirring occasionally. Add the peas and stock and simmer for 25 minutes or until all the vegetables are tender. Remove from the heat and allow to cool. Sieve or liquidise the vegetables and return to the pan. Add the grilled gammon pieces, season with pepper and herbs. Return to the stove, heat thoroughly and serve hot with crusty bread.

Crab Cakes

*Horseradish sauce adds flavour to the crab cakes and
watercress adds taste and colour to the mayonnaise.*

CAKES
8 oz crab meat   1 lb cooked, mashed potatoes   1 oz butter
1 tablespoon freshly chopped parsley   1 level teaspoon creamed horseradish

COATING
2 medium eggs, beaten   3 oz golden breadcrumbs
Salt and pepper   4 tablespoons cooking oil with 1 oz butter for frying

GREEN MAYONNAISE
2 bunches watercress, washed and trimmed   ¼ pint mayonnaise
1 clove garlic, peeled and crushed   1 tablespoon lemon juice
¼ pint natural yoghurt   Salt and pepper

In a bowl, mix together all the ingredients for the crab cakes. Divide into 12 portions and shape into rounds 1 inch thick. Dip into the beaten egg and coat with breadcrumbs. Chill in the refrigerator for at least 1 hour, then heat the oil in a frying pan, add the butter and cook the cakes for 3 to 4 minutes on each side until golden brown. Put all the ingredients for the mayonnaise into a food processor and blend until smooth. Serve the cakes hot with the mayonnaise and a fresh green salad or green vegetables.

On Bere Heath
"Egdon Heath" in the Wessex novels

Dorset Tea Bread

A really fruity wheatmeal tea bread which resembles a boiled fruit cake.

1 cup of tea (no milk)   6 oz butter   8 oz soft brown sugar
12 oz mixed dried fruit (can include some walnuts, if liked)
12 oz self-raising wheatmeal flour
1 teaspoon ground mixed spice   1 teaspoon ground cinnamon
3 medium eggs, beaten

Set oven to 325°F or Mark 3. Grease and line an 8 inch round cake tin. Put the tea, butter, sugar and fruit into a saucepan and simmer gently for 15 minutes until the fruit is plump. Remove from the heat, allow to cool slightly and beat in the flour, spices and eggs. Put into the cake tin and bake for 2 hours until cooked through and a skewer inserted comes out clean. Cool and serve plain or buttered.

Gooseberry Fool

A creamy mid-summer dessert.

1 lb fresh gooseberries, topped and tailed
2-4 oz caster sugar   2 tablespoons water
1 teaspoon elderflower cordial (optional)
¼ pint double cream   2½ fl.oz natural yoghurt

Put the gooseberries into a saucepan with the sugar and water. Cover and cook gently until the gooseberries are soft. Remove from the heat and allow to cool. Rub the fruit through a sieve or purée in a food processor and then sieve to remove the seeds. Stir in the elderflower cordial if desired. Whip the cream to a floppy consistency. Stir the yoghurt into the cold gooseberry purée and lastly fold in the cream. Spoon into 4 individual sundae dishes and serve with crisp sweet biscuits or sponge finger biscuits.

Vegetable Hot Pot with Cheesy Dumplings

Mixed vegetables make this vegetarian casserole dish.

**2 oz butter   2 medium onions, peeled and sliced
2 cloves garlic, peeled and crushed   1 oz plain flour   1 pint vegetable stock
¼ pint white wine   2 medium parsnips, cut into ¼ inch slices
3 large carrots, cut into ¼ inch slices   2 sticks celery, cut into ¼ inch slices
8 oz tinned red kidney beans (drained)   8 oz button mushrooms, wiped
½ teaspoon dried mixed herbs   Salt and pepper**

DUMPLINGS
**4 oz self-raising flour   1 oz butter, softened   2 oz Cheddar cheese, grated
1 level teaspoon dried mustard powder   Cold water**

Set oven to 350°F or Mark 4. Melt the butter in a large pan, add the onions and garlic and cook gently until soft. Stir in the flour and cook for 2 to 3 minutes. Remove from the heat and stir in the stock and wine. Add all the remaining ingredients, season and transfer to a large casserole dish. Cover and cook in the oven for 1 hour. Make the dumplings: put the flour into a bowl, rub in the butter and stir in the cheese and mustard and enough cold water to make a soft, but not sticky dough. Divide into about 10 balls and drop into the casserole and continue cooking, covered, for a further 20 to 30 minutes. Serve hot. Serves 4 to 6.

Dorset Apple Cake

*This simple-to-make cake can be served warm with cream or custard as a pudding,
or cold spread with butter for tea.*

8 oz self-raising flour   4 oz butter, softened
4 oz caster sugar
½ lb cooking apples, peeled, cored and diced
Grated rind of one lemon
1 medium egg, beaten
2 oz sultanas (optional)

Set oven to 375°F or Mark 5. Well grease an 8 inch round cake tin. Put the
flour into a large bowl and rub in the butter until the mixture resembles
breadcrumbs. Stir in the sugar, diced apple, lemon rind and egg and mix well.
Add and stir in the sultanas, if desired. Put the mixture into the cake tin and
bake for 30 to 40 minutes until golden in colour.

Bere Regis
"Kingsbere" in *Tess of the D'Urbervilles*

Poached Eggs with Watercress Sauce

A light lunch or supper dish of poached eggs in watercress sauce,
covered with a cheesy topping.

4 large farm fresh eggs

SAUCE
2 oz butter   2 bunches watercress, trimmed, washed and chopped
1 small onion, peeled and diced   ½ pint milk
1 oz plain flour   Salt and pepper
¼ teaspoon ground nutmeg   1 oz Cheddar cheese, grated

Melt 1 oz butter in a large frying pan, add the watercress and onion and cook gently for 3 to 4 minutes. Remove from the heat and allow to cool. Sieve or purée in a food processor, with the milk. Melt the remaining 1 oz butter in the pan, stir in the flour and cook for 3 to 4 minutes. Remove from the heat and gradually stir in the watercress milk. Return to the heat and, stirring, bring to the boil until the sauce thickens. Cook gently for 3 to 4 minutes. Season with salt, pepper and a little nutmeg. Meanwhile poach the eggs until only just set. Place them in a shallow, ovenproof dish, cover with the sauce, sprinkle with cheese and brown quickly under a very hot grill. Serve hot with fresh, crusty bread. Serves 4.

Pear and Ginger Upside-down Pudding

*This pudding is delicious served with a sauce made by mixing together
equal quantities of natural yoghurt and whipped double cream.*

TOPPING
2 oz butter   4 oz soft brown sugar
1 medium can pears in natural juice (approximately 4 pears)
8-12 walnut halves

6 oz plain flour	**3 oz butter**
1 teaspoon bicarbonate of soda	**4 oz soft brown sugar**
½ teaspoon salt	**4 oz black treacle**
1 teaspoon ground ginger	**¼ pint milk**

1 medium egg, beaten

Set oven to 350°F or Mark 4. First prepare the topping. Cream together the
butter and sugar in a bowl and spread evenly over the base of an 8 inch
diameter deep cake tin. Arrange the pear halves on top (cut side down) and
place the walnuts attractively around them. Next, put the flour, bicarbonate of
soda, salt, ginger and cinnamon into a large bowl. Heat together the butter,
sugar and treacle in a saucepan until the butter has melted, but do not boil. Stir
in the milk and egg. Beat the liquid ingredients into the flour until smooth and
pour over the pears. Bake for approximately 1 hour. Turn out and serve warm.

Portland across Weymouth Bay
The "Isle of Slingers" in the Wessex novels

Shellfish Soup

This recipe takes advantage of the range of frozen shellfish which is available;
fresh shellfish can be used where possible.

2 tablespoons olive oil   2 medium onions, peeled and diced
2 cloves of garlic, peeled and crushed
1 tin chopped tomatoes with basil   ½ pint dry white wine
12 oz mixed shellfish; mussels, scallops, prawns etc (defrost if frozen)

Heat the oil in a large saucepan and soften the onions and garlic. Add the tinned tomatoes and the wine and cook for 5 minutes. Add the shellfish and cook for a further 5 minutes. Serve piping hot with crusty bread.

Gooseberry and Elderflower Jelly

*Elderflower complements the taste of gooseberries very well,
but sage or mint may be used as an alternative.*

4 lb gooseberries, washed
Granulated sugar, (1 lb to every pint of juice)
Sprigs of elderflowers, sage or mint (tied in a piece of muslin)

Put the gooseberries into a large, thick based pan with just enough water to cover them. Simmer until the fruit is very soft. Strain through a jelly bag (it is best to leave it dripping overnight). Do not squeeze the bag or a cloudy jelly will result. Measure the juice and return to the pan with 1 lb sugar for every pint of liquid. Stir over a low heat until the sugar is dissolved, put the muslin bag containing the elderflowers etc. into the liquid and boil rapidly until setting point is reached. Test by putting a little on a cold plate, leave to cool and if the surface wrinkles when a finger is pushed across it, the jelly is ready. Remove the muslin bag, skim off any scum, pot into clean, warm jars and cover. Makes 3 to 4 lb of jelly.

Lamb Steaks with Redcurrant Sauce

The rosemary marinade adds flavour to the meat before grilling.

4 lamb steaks, cut across the leg

MARINADE
¼ pint red wine
1 onion, peeled and roughly chopped
2-3 sprigs of rosemary
6 peppercorns
1 tablespoon olive oil

4 tablespoons redcurrant jelly
Sprigs of rosemary to garnish

Put the marinade ingredients into a small saucepan and heat until almost boiling. Leave to get completely cold. Put the lamb steaks into a shallow dish and pour the marinade over; cover and leave in a cool place for 3 to 4 hours. When ready, remove the meat, strain the marinade and put the liquid into a small pan. Add the redcurrant jelly and stir over a gentle heat until the jelly melts. Grill the lamb steaks, as preferred, under a hot grill. Serve with warm redcurrant sauce and garnish with fresh rosemary sprigs. Serves 4.

Dorchester Scone Ring

*Cheese scones made with wheatmeal flour and baked together
in the form of an overlapping circle.*

8 oz self-raising wheatmeal flour	**2 oz butter, softened**
1 teaspoon baking powder	**4 oz Cheddar cheese, grated**
½ teaspoon salt	**¼ pint milk**
1 teaspoon dry English mustard powder	**1 small beaten egg, to glaze**
2 level teaspoons poppy seeds	

Set oven to 425°F or Mark 7. Put the flour, baking powder, salt and mustard powder into a bowl. Rub the butter into the dry ingredients, add the cheese and mix in enough milk to make a soft dough. Turn on to a floured surface, roll to ½ inch thickness and cut out into about eight 2½ inch round scones with a pastry cutter. On a lightly floured baking sheet arrange the scones in a circle, with each scone overlapping the next one slightly. Brush with egg, sprinkle with poppy seeds and bake for approximately 15 to 20 minutes until golden brown. Cool on a wire rack. Serve split and buttered.

Wool
"Wellbridge" in *Tess of the D'Urbervilles*

Gardener's Pie

Courgettes are the basis of this vegetable crumble,
which has cheese and mixed nuts in the topping.

3 tablespoons walnut oil   2 onions, peeled and sliced
3 cloves of garlic, peeled and crushed
2 lb courgettes, washed, trimmed and cut into ½ inch slices
1 lb tomatoes, skinned and chopped   2 tablespoons tomato purée
3 or 4 basil leaves, chopped   Salt and pepper

TOPPING
3 oz fresh brown breadcrumbs
2 oz Cheddar cheese, grated
2 oz chopped mixed nuts

Set oven to 350°F or Mark 4. Heat the oil in a large saucepan, add the onions and garlic and cook gently for 5 minutes. Add all the remaining ingredients, season and cook for a further 5 minutes. Turn into a 3 pint ovenproof dish. Topping: mix together the topping ingredients and sprinkle evenly over the vegetables. Cook in the oven for about 30 minutes. Serve hot with crusty bread. Serves 4.

Digestive Biscuits

These biscuits are excellent with Dorset Blue Vinney Cheese.

6 oz self-raising wholemeal flour	**3 oz butter, softened**
2 oz fine oatmeal	**1 oz soft brown sugar**
1 level teaspoon salt	**4 tablespoons milk**

Set oven to 375°F or Mark 5. Put the flour, oatmeal and salt into a bowl and rub in the butter until the mixture resembles breadcrumbs. Stir in the sugar and enough milk to bind to a firm dough. Roll out on a floured surface to ¼ inch thickness. Cut into 3 inch rounds with a pastry cutter and prick evenly all over with a fork. Transfer to a floured baking sheet and bake for approximately 20 minutes until lightly browned. Cool slightly before transferring to a wire rack. Serve plain or buttered with cheese.

The Saxon Church, Wareham
"Anglebury" in the Wessex novels

Wareham Bears

*These biscuits can be made either with a plain shortbread or
a chocolate shortbread mixture, as desired..*

5 oz plain flour   1 oz cornflour
OR
5½ oz plain flour   ½ oz cocoa powder

4 oz butter, cut into small pieces
2 oz caster sugar   2 tablespoons milk
Currants and glacé cherries for decoration

Set oven to 325°F or Mark 3. Sieve the flour and cornflour OR flour and cocoa powder into a large bowl. Add the butter and rub into the flour until the mixture resembles breadcrumbs. Stir in the sugar, add the milk and bind the mixture together by hand to form a ball of dough. Roll out the dough to ¼ inch thickness on a lightly floured surface. Cut out shapes with a bear-shaped pastry cutter and transfer to a lightly floured baking sheet. Decorate with currants and pieces of glacé cherry to make eyes, nose etc. Bake for 30 minutes until pale golden. Cool on the baking sheet for 5 minutes before transferring to a wire rack.

Nutty Baked Cabbage

A tasty way of cooking white cabbage with a cheesy flavoured nutty sauce.

1 small white cabbage, trimmed and roughly chopped
1 oz butter   1 oz plain flour   ½ pint milk
4 oz Cheddar cheese, grated   4 oz chopped mixed nuts
Salt and pepper

Set oven to 425°F or Mark 7. Butter a shallow 2 pint ovenproof dish. Put the cabbage into a pan of boiling, salted water and cook until only just tender. Meanwhile make the sauce: melt the butter in a saucepan, stir in the flour and cook for 2 to 3 minutes. Remove from the heat and stir in the milk. Return to the heat and, stirring, bring to the boil until the sauce thickens; simmer for 5 minutes. Add the cheese and season well. Arrange layers of the cabbage, sauce and chopped nuts in the dish, finishing with a layer of sauce with a sprinkling of nuts. Bake in the oven for 20 minutes. Serve as a dish on its own or as an accompaniment to meat.

Apple and Blueberry Eve's Pudding

A layered fruit base finished with a sponge topping.

3 medium cooking apples, peeled, cored and sliced
8 oz blueberries, topped and tailed
3 oz caster sugar

TOPPING
3 oz butter   3 oz caster sugar   1 medium egg, beaten
4 oz self-raising flour   Grated rind of a lemon
2 tablespoons milk

Set oven to 350°F or Mark 4. Butter a 1½ pint ovenproof dish. Arrange in the dish layers of apples, blueberries and sugar. For the topping, cream the butter and sugar together in a bowl until pale and stir in the beaten egg, a little at a time. Fold in the flour, lemon rind and milk. Spread this mixture evenly over the fruit and bake for 45 minutes until the apples and sponge are cooked through. Serve warm with cream or custard.

Crab Tart

A crab meat and spring onion quiche, served warm or cold, garnished with watercress.

8 oz shortcrust pastry

FILLING
4 oz cream cheese
1 medium egg   ¼ pint single cream
2 teaspoons lemon juice
Salt and pepper
½-¾ lb crab meat (mixture of white and brown meat)
4 spring onions, trimmed, washed and cut into ¼ inch slices
Watercress to garnish

Set oven to 400°F or Mark 6. Roll out the pastry on a lightly floured surface and use to line a greased 8 inch flan ring. Prick the base with a fork, line with kitchen foil, and bake for 10 to 15 minutes. Remove the foil. For the filling, put the cream cheese into a large bowl and beat until soft. Mix in the egg, cream, lemon juice and seasoning. Arrange the crab meat and spring onions over the base of the flan and pour over the cheese mixture. Reduce oven to 375°F or Mark 5 and bake for 30 to 40 minutes until set and golden.

An Old Corner, West Bay
Thomas Hardy's "Port Bredy"

Uncle Bert's Apple Chutney

A useful way of using up a surfeit of cooking apples; ideal for windfalls.
Makes approximately 4 lb chutney.

3 lb cooking apples, peeled, cored and diced
3 medium onions, peeled and diced
1 lb soft brown sugar   ½ pint malt vinegar
2 cloves of garlic, peeled and crushed
1 lb sultanas   2 teaspoons curry powder
2 teaspoons ground ginger

Put the apples, onions, sugar and vinegar in a large saucepan. Bring to the boil, reduce the heat and simmer for approximately 15 minutes until the mixture is pulpy. Add all the remaining ingredients and simmer until the mixture is reduced to a thick consistency, with no excess liquid. Pot into clean, warm jars. Cover, seal and label.

Chicken and Field Mushroom Pie

A simple pie using left-oven cooked chicken.

8 oz shortcrust pastry
1 oz butter   1 medium onion, peeled and diced
1 oz plain flour   ½ pint chicken stock
2 tablespoons dry white wine or sherry
6 oz field mushrooms, wiped and sliced
1 lb cooked chicken, cut into small pieces
Salt and pepper

Set oven to 400°F or Mark 6. Melt the butter in a pan, add the onion and cook gently until soft. Add the flour and, stirring, cook for 2 to 3 minutes. Remove from the heat and gradually stir in the stock and sherry. Return to the heat and bring to the boil, stirring, until the sauce thickens. Add the mushrooms and simmer for 5 minutes. Stir in the chicken pieces and season well. Put the mixture into a 2 pint pie dish. Roll out the pastry on a lightly floured surface and use to cover the dish. Cut a hole in the pastry lid to allow the steam to escape and bake for approximately 30 minutes until golden brown. Serve hot. Serves 4.

Lulworth Cove
"Lulstead Cove" in *Far from the Madding Crowd*

Old Harry Rock Cakes

An extra spicy, fruity variety of rock cake.

8 oz self-raising wheatmeal flour
½ teaspoon mixed spice   ½ teaspoon ground cinnamon
4 oz butter, softened   4 oz Demerara sugar
4 oz mixed dried fruit
(currants, sultanas, mixed peel, glacé cherries etc. in any proportion)
Grated rind of half a lemon   1 medium egg, beaten
2 tablespoons milk

Set oven to 375°F or Mark 5. Sift the flour, mixed spice and cinnamon together into a bowl and rub in the butter until the mixture resembles breadcrumbs. Stir in the sugar, dried fruit and lemon rind. Add the egg and milk and combine with the dry ingredients to form a crumbly dough. Form into 10 or 12 rough heaps on a greased baking tray. Bake for approximately 20 minutes until lightly browned. Cool on the baking tray for 5 minutes before transferring to a wire rack. These cakes are best eaten on the same day as made; they freeze well.

Dorset Dough Cake

*This resembles a large currant bun and is best eaten when very fresh,
traditionally without butter.*

BREAD DOUGH
**8 oz strong white plain flour   ½ teaspoon salt   ⅓ oz butter or lard
1 teaspoon dried yeast   5 fl.oz warm water**

ADDITIVES
**2 oz butter, softened   2 oz caster sugar
4 oz mixed dried fruit   1-2 teaspoons mixed spice**

Well grease a 6 inch round cake tin. Make 12 oz of bread dough, well-kneaded
in the normal manner, cover with a clean tea towel and set aside in the warm to
rise. When it has doubled in bulk, place on a floured surface and knock back.
Then spread or roll out, dot with the butter and fold and work it into the dough.
Repeat with the sugar, fruit and spice, kneading and blending until everything
is well incorporated; this results in a somewhat sticky dough. Put the dough in
the tin, smooth the top, cover and set aside to rise. As this is a rich mixture it
may take 1 to 1½ hours to rise nearly to the top of the tin. Set oven to 400°F
or Mark 6 and, when the dough has risen, bake for 30 to 40 minutes, covering
with greaseproof paper if it is browning too quickly. When done, turn out on
to a wire rack and brush the top with warm sugar syrup or honey to glaze.

Lyme Bay Fish Pie

A luxury fish pie filling topped with filo pastry; not at all like an ordinary fish pie.

8 oz filo pastry   2 oz butter   6 spring onions, trimmed and sliced
4 oz mushrooms, wiped and sliced   1 oz plain flour
½ pint fish stock   ¼ pint dry white wine
8 oz white fish fillets, skinned and cut into pieces
8 oz scallops   8 oz prawns, cooked and peeled (thaw if frozen)
4 tomatoes, skinned, de-seeded and cut into strips
1 tablespoon chopped parsley   Salt and pepper

Set oven to 375°F or Mark 5. Melt 1 oz butter in a large frying pan and gently cook the onions and mushrooms for 3 to 4 minutes. Stir in the flour and cook for 2 to 3 minutes. Remove from the heat and add the stock gradually, stirring well all the time. Stir in the wine. Return to the heat and bring to the boil; cook for 3 to 4 minutes. Remove from the heat and add the fish pieces, scallops, prawns, tomatoes and parsley. Season and put into a shallow ovenproof dish. Melt the remaining butter in a small pan. Arrange the sheets of filo pastry on top of the fish, brushing each layer with melted butter. Trim the pastry and score the surface into diamond shapes. Cook for 25 to 30 minutes until golden. Serve hot. Serves 4.

METRIC CONVERSIONS

The weights, measures and oven temperatures used in the preceding recipes can be easily converted to their metric equivalents. The conversions listed below are only approximate, having been rounded up or down as may be appropriate.

Weights

Avoirdupois	Metric
1 oz.	just under 30 grams
4 oz. (¼ lb.)	app. 115 grams
8 oz. (½ lb.)	app. 230 grams
1 lb.	454 grams

Liquid Measures

Imperial	Metric
1 tablespoon (liquid only)	20 millilitres
1 fl. oz.	app. 30 millilitres
1 gill (¼ pt.)	app. 145 millilitres
½ pt.	app. 285 millilitres
1 pt.	app. 570 millilitres
1 qt.	app. 1.140 litres

Oven Temperatures

	°Fahrenheit	Gas Mark	°Celsius
Slow	300	2	150
	325	3	170
Moderate	350	4	180
	375	5	190
	400	6	200
Hot	425	7	220
	450	8	230
	475	9	240

Flour as specified in these recipes refers to plain flour unless otherwise described.